TAKING CYSTIC FIBROSIS TO SCHOOL

JayJo Books, L.L.C.

Publishing Special Books for Special Kids®

P.O. Box 213
Valley Park, MO 63088-0213

Published by
JayJo Books, L.L.C.
P.O. Box 213
Valley Park, MO 63088-0213

Edited by Kim Gosselin

Library of Congress Cataloging-In-Publication Data
Henry, Cynthia S.
Taking Cystic Fibrosis To School/Cynthia S. Henry-First Edition
Library of Congress Catalog Card Number 00-190097
1.Health Education
2.Children's Disabilities
3.Non-Fiction

ISBN 1-891383-09-4
Library of Congress
7th book in our *"Special Kids in School"*® series.

*All books printed by JayJo Books, L.L.C. are available at special quantity discounts when purchased in bulk. Special imprints, logos, messages and excerpts can be designed to meet your needs. For more information call the publisher at 636-861-1331 or fax at 636-861-2411. E-mail us at jayjobooks@aol.com.

Dedication
To my children, Alex and Chase, with hopes for a healthy and happy future.

About the author:

Cynthia S. Henry was born and raised in Lancaster County, Pennsylvania. She attended Shippensburg University. Cynthia now lives in Lancaster County with her husband and their two children.

Cynthia's particular interest in children's health issues began when her son, Chase, was diagnosed with a peanut allergy and asthma. Since then, she has written about food allergies and other children's health concerns. She is committed to bringing awareness to children's health issues, as well as educating others.

Hi! My name is Jessie. I have a mom, a dad, and a sister, Christine. Oh yeah, and my dog. His name is Buddy. All of us are special for lots of different reasons. I'm a good friend, a good kid, and a good sister. I can run really fast! I love to read books and my family loves me a whole lot too!

1'm extra special though, because I have cystic fibrosis. Cystic fibrosis (CF) means that my lungs may have trouble getting air in and out of my body. When we breathe in, we can feel our lungs fill up with air. When we breathe out, we empty our lungs. Everybody needs their lungs to work the right way to live healthy and happy lives.

Having cystic fibrosis means that my lungs sometimes get covered with sticky mucus. Try to think of a spider web that catches germs, instead of flies. The mucus in my lungs is like a spider web. It traps the germs. That's bad. The germs make me sick!

When my chest gets tight from the mucus, it feels like there are great big elephants dancing on it! To make me feel better, I cough and cough and cough! At first, the other kids in school didn't understand why I had to cough so much. Coughing helps to clear my lungs. If you hear me coughing a lot, please help me by telling the teacher or the school nurse.

My doctors and nurses told me that cystic fibrosis was something I inherited from the genes in my body. Genes are the things in our bodies that makes us who we are! Genes are in everyone's body!

The shape of our noses, our hands, and even our feet come from our genes! Genes give us eye color and hair color too! Some genes are good and some are bad. Usually, nobody knows what genes we're going to get until after we're born.

Like all kids, I have to take very good care of my body. I like to eat foods that are best for me. Fruits, vegetables, chicken, and fish are some of my very favorites! I also have to make sure that I get lots of sleep--no staying up past bedtime for me!!

Unlike most kids, even a small cold can be very bad for me! To help keep my lungs clear, my mom and dad pat my back every day. I lie on my belly on a special board that is slanted. My mom and dad pat, pat, pat, my back to help me breathe easier. They make up silly songs and stories to help me feel better while they're doing it. The patting really does help get rid of that yucky mucus!

One time I got a cold that went into my chest. I had to go to the hospital. I was kind of scared. But, the nurses and doctors were so nice to me! They hooked me up to a machine that helped me breathe easier. They called the machine "Betty". Betty was like a vest that vibrated my lungs to shake out all of the bad mucus. It felt really funny!

The nurses and doctors gave me lots of good food to eat. I even got ice cream and pudding! Lots of people came to see me. My friends even sent me special cards they had made for me at school!

Sometimes I have to use a nebulizer machine. The nebulizer machine helps get special medicine deep into my lungs where it works best. Usually, after I use my nebulizer machine, I can do almost anything! I like to play soccer, dance, and visit with my friends.

Kids with cystic fibrosis may need air purifiers in their bedrooms, too. An air purifier is a small machine that keeps the air super clean! I have one! The machine helps me to stay healthy, and breathe easier while I'm sleeping.

Doctors and nurses say it's good for me to get lots of air into my lungs! I do that by dancing, jumping, running, and laughing; just like any other kid! My lungs may not always work the way they should, but my heart is very, very, BIG!

THE END

LET'S TAKE THE CYSTIC FIBROSIS KIDS QUIZ!

1. **How do lungs work?**
   Lungs take air in and out of our bodies and send it to other parts of our bodies to make them work.

2. **What happens to your lungs when you have cystic fibrosis?**
   CF affects many parts of my body. Sometimes, my lungs get a sticky mucus that traps bad germs.

3. **Is CF contagious?**
   No. You can still play with me and be my friend. You can't catch cystic fibrosis from me or anyone else.

4. **Do you have a special diet?**
   No, but I try to eat healthy foods. It's a diet that's good for anyone!

5. **Why do you cough so much?**
   Coughing can help make it easier for me to breathe. The coughing helps get the mucus out of my lungs.

6. **When do you have to go to the hospital?**
   I have to go to the hospital when the things we do at home are not working right. The doctors and nurses watch closely to make sure that I don't get any sicker.

7. **Can you exercise and play sports?**
   Yes! Exercise is one of the best ways to treat cystic fibrosis.

TEN TIPS FOR TEACHERS

✓ **1. EACH CHILD LIVING WITH CYSTIC FIBROSIS IS UNIQUE.**
Each child living with CF has different symptoms. Common symptoms of
CF include excessive coughing, poor weight gain and/or delayed growth,
wheezing, pneumonia, and fatigue.

✓ **2. BE PREPARED TO PROVIDE SUPPORT AND MATERIALS
DURING HOSPITAL STAYS.**
Hospital stays are a fact of life for many children living with CF. Try to help
the child keep up with his or her homework when hospitalized.

✓ **3. TRY TO PROVIDE HELP WITH MEDICATION, VITAMINS,
OR TREATMENTS, IF NECESSARY.**
There are times when the student living with CF will have to take antibiotics, extra
vitamins/enzymes, or even use a nebulizer machine. Talk to the school nurse and give
gentle, friendly reminders to your student when necessary. Try passing a note or
using a "secret code"!

✓ **4. WATCH FOR SIGNS THAT YOUR STUDENT'S HEALTH
MAY BE DETERIORATING.**
Excessive coughing and weakness are two noticeable signs that may indicate your student
living with CF is having trouble. Tell the school nurse and/or the parents right away if
you notice any abnormal symptoms.

✓ **5. COMMUNICATE WITH YOUR STUDENT'S PARENTS,
CAREGIVERS, DOCTORS, AND NURSES.**
The key to working with a child living with CF is communication.
You are an important part of his or her **TEAM**. You should expect
parents to tell you about any changes in symptoms they have
noticed, and you should communicate the same to them.

6. LISTEN TO YOUR STUDENT LIVING WITH CF.

Your student living with CF has a life full of special feelings. All of the issues that are involved with CF including illness, treatments, and even possible death can be overwhelming to a child. Sometimes they just need to talk. Open your heart to them and be their mentor.

7. ENCOURAGE OPEN DISCUSSION IN THE CLASSROOM ABOUT CYSTIC FIBROSIS.

Having a child living with CF in your classroom can be a rewarding experience. Because of the nature of this disease, those diagnosed with CF often have unique and very inspirational views of life. Allow this to become part of your classroom and encourage your students to share their feelings.

8. BE CONSCIENTIOUS ABOUT GERMS.

Keep in mind that children living with CF are more susceptible to bad germs (colds, coughs, etc.). It's important that safe and sanitary habits are encouraged in the classroom.

9. KEEP AN OPEN MIND.

This may be your first experience relating to a child living with CF. Even if it is not, each child is different in the way his or her body reacts to their condition. Please be open-minded and patient! You will be rewarded greatly!

10. TREAT YOUR STUDENT LIVING WITH CF AS SOMEONE SPECIAL, JUST LIKE ALL OF THE OTHER STUDENTS IN YOUR CLASS.

Your student living with CF wants to be treated like all the other children in the classroom! He or she doesn't want to feel any "different" than any of the other students!